W9-AVX-889

SHOCKWAVE
SCIENCE

Mighty Earth

© 2008 Weldon Owen Education Inc. All rights reserved.

No part of this publication may be reproduced or transmitted
in any form or by any means, electronic or mechanical,
including photocopying, recording, taping, or any information storage
and retrieval system, without permission in writing from the publisher.

Library of Congress Cataloging-in-Publication Data

Allison, Carol J.
   Mighty earth / by Carol J. Allison.
      p. cm. -- (Shockwave)
   Includes index.
   ISBN-10: 0-531-17794-7 (lib. bdg.)
   ISBN-13: 978-0-531-17794-5 (lib. bdg.)
   ISBN-10: 0-531-15482-3 (pbk.)
   ISBN-13: 978-0-531-15482-3 (pbk.)
 1. Earth sciences--Juvenile literature. 2. Earth--Juvenile literature.
I. Title. II. Series.
   QE29.A535 2008
   550--dc22

2007012228

Published in 2008 by Children's Press, an imprint of Scholastic Inc.,
557 Broadway, New York, New York 10012
www.scholastic.com

SCHOLASTIC, CHILDREN'S PRESS, and associated logos are trademarks
and/or registered trademarks of Scholastic Inc.

08 09 10 11 12 13 14 15 16 17
10 9 8 7 6 5 4 3 2 1

Printed in China through Colorcraft Ltd., Hong Kong

Author: Carol J. Allison
Educational Consultant: Ian Morrison
Editor: Nerida Frost
Designer: Miguel Carvajal
Photo Researcher: Jamshed Mistry

Photographs by: Big Stock Photo (p. 34); **Brand X Pictures** (coral, p. 27); **Corel** (p. 17);
Getty Images (pp. 8–9); **Jennifer and Brian Lupton** (teenagers, pp. 32–33); **John Foxx
Images** (p. 3; p. 5); **Photodisc** (p. 18); © **Robert Preston/Alamy** (p. 12); **Tranz/Corbis**
(cover; p. 7; pp. 10–11; pp. 13–16; pp. 19–26; bleached coral, p. 27; p. 28; pp. 30–31;
Everglades housing development, pp. 32–33); **www.saasta.ac.za** (p. 29)

All illustrations and other photographs © Weldon Owen Education Inc.

Mighty Earth

Carol J. Allison

children's press®

An imprint of Scholastic Inc.

NEW YORK • TORONTO • LONDON • AUCKLAND • SYDNEY
MEXICO CITY • NEW DELHI • HONG KONG
DANBURY, CONNECTICUT

CHECK THESE OUT!

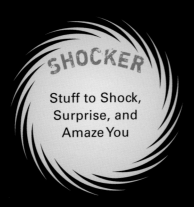

SHOCKER

Stuff to Shock,
Surprise, and
Amaze You

Quick Recaps
and Notable
Notes

Word Stunners
and Other Oddities

The Heads-Up
on Expert Reading

Links to More
Information

CONTENTS

chasm (*KA zm*) a deep crack in the earth's surface

erode to wear away land by water, ice, or wind

glacier (*GLAY shur*) a large mass of slow-moving ice

gorge (*GORJ*) a deep valley with steep, rocky sides

lava *(LA vuh)* melted rock that has come out of a volcano

magma melted rock that is inside the earth

monolithic (*mon uh LITH ik*) shaped like a monolith, which is a single massive block of stone

plate a large section of the earth's surface

plateau (*pla TOH*) an area of high, flat land

For additional vocabulary, see Glossary on page 34.

Some words can have several different meanings. Some of the other meanings of *plate* are:
• a shallow dish
• a flat sheet of metal
• a part of a denture

Tiger Leaping
Gorge,
Yangtze River,
China

The forces of nature have created great wonders on the earth. It took millions of years to form some of the world's huge mountains, and deep canyons. Vast deserts and mighty mountains were here long before humans.

Many natural wonders were formed by forces from within the earth. Others were formed by natural forces from outside, such as wind. Scientists study natural wonders in order to understand the history of our planet. Understanding the planet's history will help us to protect it. The earth's natural wonders are not simply a clue to our past. They are also a clue to our future.

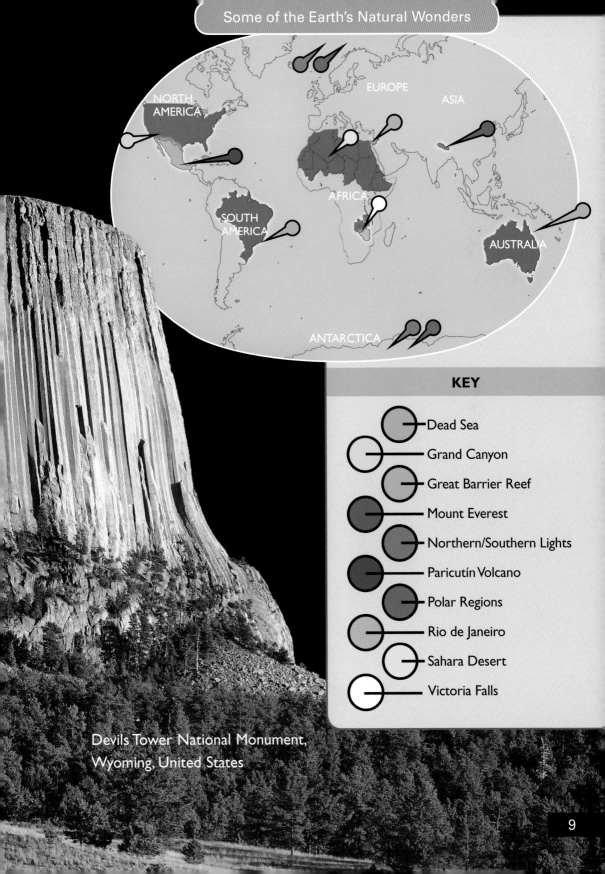

NORTH
AMERICA

EUROPE

ASIA

AFRICA

SOUTH
AMERICA

AUSTRALIA

ANTARCTICA

KEY

Dead Sea

Grand Canyon

Great Barrier Reef

Mount Everest

Northern/Southern Lights

Paricutín Volcano

Polar Regions

Rio de Janeiro

Sahara Desert

Victoria Falls

Devils Tower National Monument,
Wyoming, United States

Forces on Earth

The surface of the earth is made up of **plates**. These fit together like a giant jigsaw puzzle. They meet at cracks, called faults. When the plates slide past each other, earthquakes may occur. When the plates crash into each other, mountains and **gorges** are formed. Inside the earth, there are patches of hot, melted rock, called **magma**. When the earth's plates pull apart and magma escapes, volcanoes are created.

Marble Cave is in General Carrera Lake, Chile. Waves on the lake carved it out over thousands of years.

School bus buried in lava near Kilauea

SHOCKER

The most recent eruption of Kilauea Volcano in Hawaii started in 1983. It hasn't stopped since! **Lava** has covered 43 square miles of land, including an entire town.

I had some trouble figuring out the different types of plate movement. Rereading the paragraph and looking at the diagram helped me get a better understanding.

Forces, such as wind and water, work on the earth from the outside. Pounding waves can **erode** land to form caves. Deserts can form when water **evaporates**. Rivers cut through rocks to form waterfalls and gorges.

Natural forces sometimes cause natural disasters. Extreme weather, such as hurricanes, can change the landscape forever.

Direction of Plate Movements

Some Earthquakes

Mountain

Volcano

On Top of the World

Mount Everest, Nepal and Tibet

Imagine standing on top of the world. Many people who want to do this try to climb Mount Everest. It is the highest mountain in the world. It stands 29,035 feet high. That is nearly 9,000 feet higher than Mount McKinley in Alaska. Mount McKinley is also called Denali. It is the tallest mountain in North America.

Mount Everest is in the Himalayas. This mountain range started to form more than 50 million years ago. Two of the earth's plates crashed into each other. This pushed up the seabed between them. The plates are still moving, so Everest is still growing.

Some of the World's Highest Mountains

Feet

- 30,000
- 25,000
- 20,000
- 15,000
- 10,000
- 5,000
- Sea level

Everest 29,035

Asia

McKinley 20,320

Aconcagua 22,835

Kilimanjaro 19,340

Elbrus 18,510

Europe   Africa   North America   South America

SHOCKER

Mount Everest is not just littered with garbage. It is also littered with dead bodies! More than 180 people have died on Everest. Most of the bodies are still on the mountain.

Everest is a very difficult and dangerous mountain to climb. In 1953, Sir Edmund Hillary from New Zealand and Tenzing Norgay from Nepal became the first people to reach its **summit**. People all over the world celebrated this great achievement. Since 1953, more than 2,000 climbers have reached Mount Everest's summit. Sadly, many climbers have died in the attempt.

Birth of a Volcano

**Paricutín (*Pa ree ku TEEN*)
Volcano, Mexico**

People do not get to see the
birth of a volcano very often.
In February 1943, one of the
world's youngest volcanoes
was born near a village in Mexico.
For about a month, people had
felt small earthquakes. Then
a hole appeared in a cornfield.
The ground swelled up.
Lava came out of the cracks in the earth. In a single day,
a volcanic cone grew nearly 100 feet out of the ground.

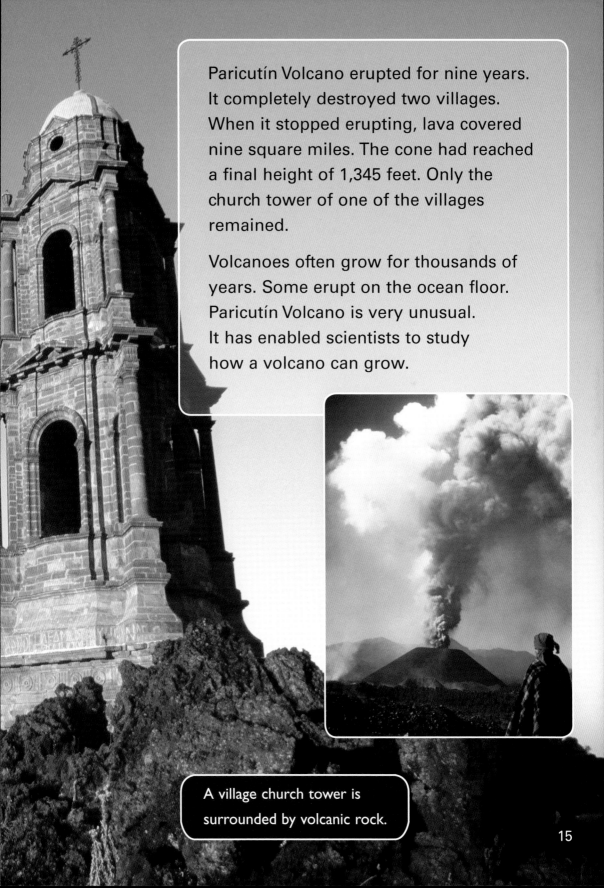

Paricutín Volcano erupted for nine years. It completely destroyed two villages. When it stopped erupting, lava covered nine square miles. The cone had reached a final height of 1,345 feet. Only the church tower of one of the villages remained.

Volcanoes often grow for thousands of years. Some erupt on the ocean floor. Paricutín Volcano is very unusual. It has enabled scientists to study how a volcano can grow.

A village church tower is surrounded by volcanic rock.

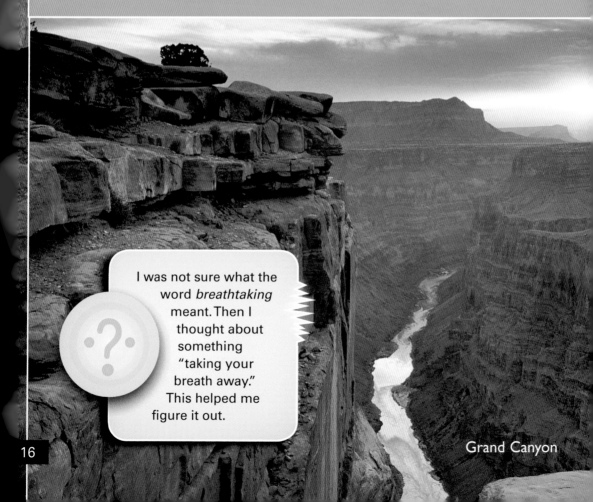

Bigger Than It Looks

Grand Canyon, United States

What was it like for the first people who stumbled upon the Grand Canyon? Imagine if you had never heard of it or seen photos of it before. It is a breathtaking sight. The Grand Canyon is 277 miles long. It is more than a mile deep. It was formed about six million years ago by the Colorado River.

I was not sure what the word *breathtaking* meant. Then I thought about something "taking your breath away." This helped me figure it out.

Grand Canyon

Did You Know?

The Grand Canyon is home to many animals, including mountain lions. Visitors must respect the animals and beware of them. Hiking is safest in groups.

Native Americans have lived in and around the Grand Canyon for thousands of years. Spanish explorers first saw it in 1540. They couldn't judge how big it was. Looking down, they thought the river below was about six feet wide. How wrong they were! In fact, the Colorado River was 300 feet wide at that point. The explorers sent men to find a way down to the river. After three days, they had to give up. They had gotten only a third of the way down the canyon!

Today, the Grand Canyon is one of the most well-known natural attractions in the world. More than five million tourists visit it each year. Since March 2007, visitors have been able to view the canyon from the Skywalk. This is a glass bridge 4,000 feet above the canyon floor.

SHOCKER

Each year, about 250 people need to be rescued from the Grand Canyon. For about ten of them, help comes too late. Some people die simply because they do not have enough water with them.

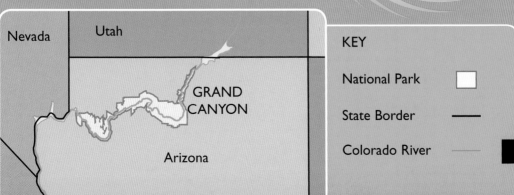

Nevada

Utah

GRAND CANYON

Arizona

KEY

National Park ☐

State Border ───

Colorado River ───

Smoke That Thunders

Victoria Falls, Zambia and Zimbabwe

The African name for Victoria Falls means "smoke that thunders."
This refers to the mist and noise that the falls make.
Victoria Falls is more than one mile wide and 300 feet tall.
Only Iguazu Falls in South America is bigger. However,
Iguazu is made up of hundreds of small waterfalls.
Victoria Falls is the largest single curtain of water in the world.

Victoria Falls was formed by the Zambezi River millions of years ago. The river flowed across a crack in the **plateau** that got wider and wider. Finally, the crack turned into a long, narrow **chasm**. The river plunged into the chasm. The water can escape from the chasm only through one small **channel**. The full force of the water hits the far side of the chasm. This sends up mist. The mist can be seen from 30 miles away.

SHOCKER

The hippopotamuses on the Zambezi River can be very dangerous. They can move surprisingly quickly. They also bite to kill. It is believed that hippos kill more tourists in Africa than any other wild animal.

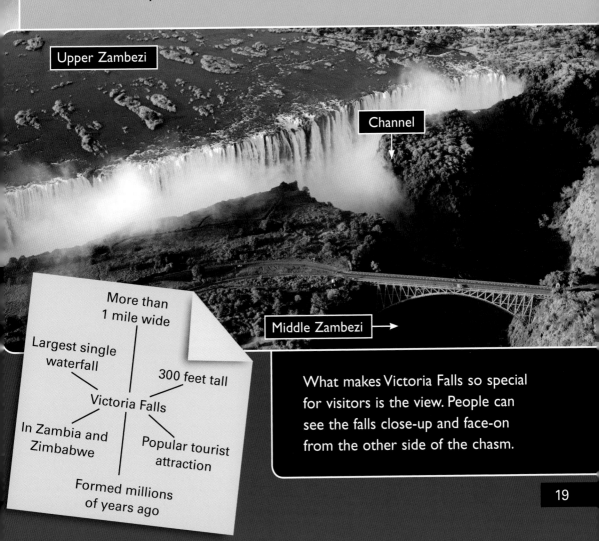

Upper Zambezi

Channel

Middle Zambezi

More than 1 mile wide

Largest single waterfall

300 feet tall

Victoria Falls

In Zambia and Zimbabwe

Popular tourist attraction

Formed millions of years ago

What makes Victoria Falls so special for visitors is the view. People can see the falls close-up and face-on from the other side of the chasm.

Dead or Dying Sea?

The Dead Sea, Israel and Jordan

Imagine reading a book while you float in the sea! People do this in the Dead Sea. There is so much salt in the sea that the water is very **dense**. This makes you float so easily that it is difficult to stand or swim.

Salt formations in the Dead Sea

SHOCKER

The Dead Sea is dying! It is drying up. As this happens, dangerous sinkholes are opening up on its shores. People have fallen into sinkholes and been injured. Large areas are no longer safe for farming and building.

Millions of years ago, the area was often flooded by the ocean. This left thick layers of salt behind. Much later, a lake formed. It was fed by the Jordan River. The lake sank to such a low level that rivers could no longer flow out of it. It became the lowest point on the surface of the earth. The only way that water could leave it was by evaporating. So the lake became saltier and saltier.

Today, the Dead Sea is nine times saltier than the ocean. No animal or plant can live in it. If a fish from the river gets into it, it soon dies. For people, however, the water of the Dead Sea is healthy. That is, if people don't drink it! It can be very good for treating skin diseases and arthritis, for example.

Mediterranean Sea

Syria

Jordan River

West Bank

Jordan

Israel

Dead Sea

The Dead Sea

Good Points:
- can relax and float
- can treat skin diseases
- helps arthritis

Bad Points:
- animals and plants can't survive
- can't swim well in it
- can't drink it

January River

Harbor of Rio de Janeiro (*REE oh day zhuh NAIR oh*), Brazil

Huge **monolithic** peaks frame the beautiful harbor. It is easy to imagine that volcanoes formed these mountains 500 million years ago. The Portuguese first saw the harbor in January 1502. Some people say they thought it was the mouth of a river. So they named it "January River" – Rio de Janeiro.

In the word *monolith*, *mono* means "one," and *lith*, from the Greek word *lithos*, means "stone."

Sugar Loaf Mountain

Did You Know?

Brazil was once a Portuguese **colony**. In 1808, the French invaded Portugal. The king of Portugal fled to Rio de Janeiro. For a few years, Rio was the capital of the Portuguese Empire. It was the only time there was a European capital outside Europe.

At the mouth of the harbor, Sugar Loaf Mountain rises almost vertically 1,325 feet out of the sea. Corcovado Mountain, behind the city, is nearly twice as high as Sugar Loaf Mountain.

Rio de Janeiro's harbor is unlike most other natural wonders of the world. It has people living all around it. Millions of tourists join them every year to enjoy Rio's exciting Carnival.

23

Seas of Sand

I already know something about deserts: that they are dry and sandy, and hot during the day. This knowledge should help me read these pages.

Jeep at the foot of a sand dune

Sahara Desert, Africa

The Sahara is the world's largest desert. It covers an area almost as big as the United States. It takes up a quarter of the **continent** of Africa. The Sahara spreads over part of ten countries. It is one of the driest places on the earth. Few plants and animals live in it. There are huge expanses of sand, known as sand seas. There are sand dunes as high as the Empire State Building! There are also rocky hills and mountains. It is very hot in the day. It can be freezing at night. Sometimes there is even snow on the mountains.

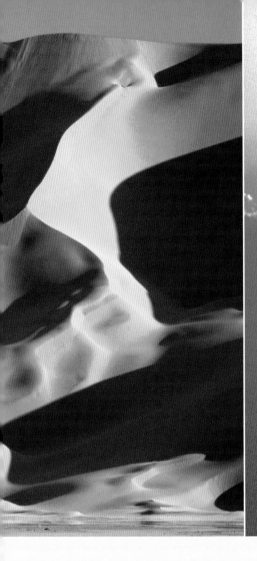

Sahara Desert

AFRICA

Did You Know?

Every year, hundreds of people come to the Sahara for "the toughest footrace on Earth." They walk or run 150 miles in six days. They endure extreme heat and cold, as well as sandstorms.

Only two million people live in the Sahara. Most of them live near one of the 90 **oases** there. In the past, some of these people, such as the Bedouins (*BEHD u ihnz*), were nomads. They spent their lives moving from oasis to oasis. Today, most of these nomads have settled in villages.

Bedouin woman and child

Underwater Treasure

Great Barrier Reef, Australia

Australia's Great Barrier Reef is the world's largest coral-reef system. It is 1,240 miles long. The reef is the largest structure made by living creatures in the world. It has a huge variety of **marine** life. Most of the reef dates back about 8,000 years. However, some of it began to form more than two million years ago!

Hard coral is made up of billions of **polyp** skeletons. Its color comes from **algae** that live inside it. Algae and hard coral need each other to survive. Warming or pollution of seawater can make the coral lose its algae. This kills the coral, turning it white. This process is known as coral bleaching. Reefs all over the world are dying from coral bleaching. In 1975, Australia set up the Great Barrier Reef Marine Park to protect this natural treasure.

KEY

Great Barrier Reef

Marine Park Limits

Great Barrier Reef

Coral Sea

AUSTRALIA

Brightly colored corals,
such as the orange cup coral,
live on healthy coral reefs.

SHOCKER

In some parts of the world,
fishermen use dynamite
to catch fish. They blow up
a reef. The fish are stunned
by the explosion. The fishermen
can then catch the fish easily.
Of course, this also
destroys the reef.

Bleached coral

Nature's Light Show

SHOCKER

During the northern lights of 1859, two **telegraph** operators in the United States were astonished. They turned off their power. However, they could still communicate. Their telegraph lines were running on solar wind power!

Northern lights, Canada

The Northern and Southern Lights, Polar Regions

The northern and southern lights are the biggest light shows on the earth. They start with a glow in the night sky. The glow grows to fill the whole sky. It can be different colors and shapes. It often looks like a huge see-through curtain rippling in a breeze.

The northern and southern lights result from solar wind. Solar wind is a high-speed flow of **particles** from the sun. The particles have an electrical charge.

The earth has a **magnetic field** that protects it from most of the solar wind. However, some of the particles get trapped by the magnetic field. They travel toward the earth's poles. As they enter the earth's **atmosphere**, they release energy in the form of light. This light can be white, red, green, blue, or violet.

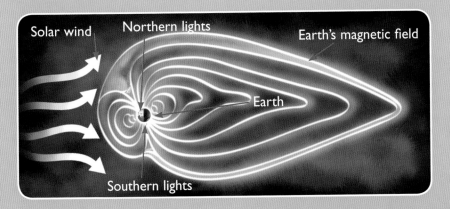

Solar wind   Northern lights   Earth's magnetic field

Earth

Southern lights

Southern lights, Antarctica

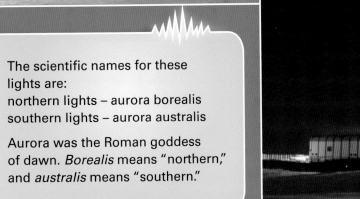

The scientific names for these lights are:
northern lights – aurora borealis
southern lights – aurora australis

Aurora was the Roman goddess of dawn. *Borealis* means "northern," and *australis* means "southern."

The Ends of the Earth

Antarctica

Polar Regions, Arctic and Antarctica

The polar regions are the coldest places on the planet. The Arctic in the north is not a piece of land. It is an ice cap that floats on the Arctic Ocean. Antarctica in the south is a frozen continent. Giant ice fields and **glaciers** cover the surface of the land. Antarctica is one of the driest places in the world.

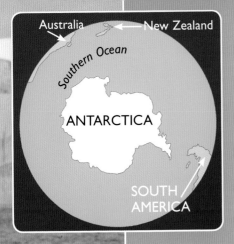

Map showing Australia, New Zealand, Southern Ocean, ANTARCTICA, SOUTH AMERICA

Map showing Edge of Arctic ice cap, 1979; Russia; Arctic ice cap, 2005; Greenland; U.S.A. (Alaska); Canada

Scientists have begun to realize just how important the polar regions are for our planet. Ice and snow act as giant reflectors. They bounce the sun's rays back into space. This keeps the planet cool enough to live on.

Scientists have observed that the polar ice caps are melting. As the ice caps melt, less sunlight is bounced back into space. Earth gets warmer. This causes even more melting. The melting water makes sea levels rise. This could cause flooding in many parts of the world.

Arctic

SHOCKER

Huge ice shelves at both poles are melting. The Larsen B Ice Shelf is in Antarctica. Scientists believe it was frozen solid for up to 12,000 years. However, in 2002, a piece the size of Rhode Island broke off.

Humans need nature to survive. We need clean air and water. We need land on which to grow food. People need the space in which to enjoy and explore nature. Nature reserves are also home to thousands of animals and plants. However, the human population is growing rapidly.

WHAT DO YOU THINK?

Should we turn more land into nature reserves and stop the spread of cities into the countryside?

PRO

We need to make sure that enough wild spaces are left for future generations to enjoy. We need to protect the land and the wildlife. We must stop housing from eating up all of our green spaces. Everybody needs an opportunity to enjoy nature.

Housing development in the Everglades, Florida

More and more land is needed for raising crops. Many people are moving out of the cities into the countryside. Plants and animals are losing their homes. We must find a balance between protecting nature and meeting the needs of an exploding population.

CON

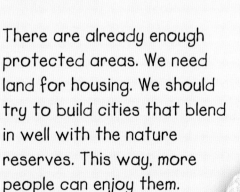

There are already enough protected areas. We need land for housing. We should try to build cities that blend in well with the nature reserves. This way, more people can enjoy them.

GLOSSARY

Algae

algae (*AL jee*) a group of simple
living things, similar to plants,
that usually live in water

atmosphere (*AT muss feer*) the mass
of gases that surround a planet

channel a narrow stretch of water between
two areas of land

colony a settlement under the rule of a parent country

continent one of the seven main land masses on the earth

dense having parts that are packed closely together

evaporate (*ee VAP uh rate*) to change from a liquid form into a gas

magnetic field the magnetic area around the earth generated
by the iron in the center of the earth

marine to do with the sea

oasis (*oh AY siss*) a place in the desert where there is water
mainly from wells or springs (plural: oases)

particle an extremely small piece of something

polyp (*PO lip*) a small sea animal with a tubular body and a round
mouth surrounded by tentacles

summit (*SUHM it*) the highest point, or top, of a mountain

telegraph a system for sending messages over long distances

FIND OUT MORE

BOOKS

Allison, Carol J. *Made by Humans: Astonishing Achievements*. Scholastic Inc., 2008.

Chester, Jonathan. *The Young Adventurer's Guide to Everest*. Tricycle Press, 2005.

Gaff, Jackie. *I Wonder Why the Sahara Is Cold at Night, and Other Questions About Deserts*. Kingfisher, 2004.

Morrison, Marion. *Rio de Janeiro*. World Almanac Library, 2004.

Sheppard, Charles. *Coral Reefs*. Voyageur Press, 2002.

WEB SITES

Go to the Web sites below to learn more about the earth.

http://volcano.und.edu

www.sio.ucsd.edu/voyager/earth_puzzle

http://library.thinkquest.org/J002388/naturalwonders.html

http://ce.eng.usf.edu/pharos/wonders/natural/index.html

INDEX

ABOUT THE AUTHOR

Having lived in many areas of the United States,
Carol J. Allison has experienced hurricanes, tornadoes,
blizzards, and earthquakes. In her travels, she has visited
massive waterfalls, giant sand dunes, deep canyons, and
huge mountains. The awesome powers of the earth's forces
fascinate her. As an author of fiction and nonfiction books
for children, Carol encourages students to learn more about
the ever-changing planet and the ways we can all work
to protect our fragile Earth.